CUPID'S CARRYING A 45

ERIK BELMER

Copyright © 2020 ERIK BELMER

Cover Art by Matt Sohl

All rights reserved.

ISBN: 9798646121999

CUPIDS CARRYING A 45

CONTENTS

The Faucet..3

Hidden Passion..4

The Path..6

Leviathan...7

Yesterday's Mo(u)ring..9

Black Rose...11

Don't Burn the Pages..12

Anxiety...13

Sparks..15

Rogue Clothes...16

The Poet...17

After Party..18

Bipolar..19

Long Forgotten Feelings...20

The Reincarnate..22

Memorial..24

And So, The World Burns.......................................25

Absolution..26

Dystopian Senses...27

Vice Grip...28

Hank Moody..30

The Note..31

Arm's Length..32

The Game...33

Ugly World..34

Christmas Present..35

Poisoned Sands...37

The Glass Remembers..39

Scenario Brain...40

Adorations Fall..42

The In-Between...43

The Passed by Looking Glass..45

Saturn Rising..48

My Pictures Face Up..50

Family Mirror..52

6 Month Killer...53

Winters Caress..54

Second Choice..55

Earned Throne..56

Heart of the Run..58

Succubus in My Mind..59

Queen of Disarray...61

The Unborn..62

Our Little Monster..64

Dishes...66

Banana Pancakes...67

Different Exits...68

Fingerprint...70

Touch Topography..71

A Poem Goodnight...72

About The Poet...73

Cupid's Carrying A 45

"Never to suffer would never to have been blessed"

-Edgar Allan Poe

The Faucet

Maybe it happened after I almost died
When I was in the in-between
My emotions seem to be pouring out of me
Like I tapped into the reservoir of the universe
And left the handle turned

I feel too much
My soul it's not escaping
It's glued to my skin
For all to see

I hope the world can handle it
I'm not sure I can

Hidden Passion

You gave me all the ammunition
But didn't tell me where to aim
It speaks volumes that all silent shots still need a fucking name
Every day I wake up they're still ringing through my brain
The sting on the pavement of my empty shells
Hidden passion labeled on the casings
That makes me feel a bewildered sort of disdain

Learning through vision and hands on experience
I'm good at anything with a bit of practice
But nothing jumps off the page
Everything feels like a lackluster distraction

My diploma just gathers dust
As the image I created
To be better than my creators
Just immediately oxidizes to rust

But now I'm slinging drinks
Filling the gills of homosapien fishes
It's not about wealth and living lavishly
It's about finding pride in purpose
To fill this abysmal void with something satisfactory

Believe it or not, I may have found it on mistake
Crafting these words
Putting soft black ink on coarse white paper
Just to make you all think beyond daily life
And the cycle of our mundane existence

The flood gates of my mind burst open
A torrent of pent up emotions and ideas
Exploded out and returned to a silent, colorless room
Releasing vibrant hues and ambient tones of lost communication

The rewards of fortuitous labor are too trivial
To quell questions of destiny and purpose

Cupid's Carrying A 45

A skydive out of a passenger window
Left me walking between two worlds
Increasing pressure on jigsaw pieces that never fit
The words hidden passion labeled on the shells
Will blow my puzzle to bits

The Path

Twenty-eight years relive the eyes of reflection.
(Bury him in the deepest of graves,
To hinder his long walk of death,
To keep the memories, close to your chest.)
In the alcove of life's doorway, I knelt like a maker,
Praying this mandatory path would show me my way.
By the frigid, wet rain and whipping winds,
Of a sky full of rage and sorrow,
Painted gray and ominous, for what lay ahead.
I spoke the calmest words of positive memories,
To uphold the man that helped shape me.

Adorned in black, the stirring stride begun,
On my own, truly abandoned, my journey began.
In the only direction I've ever known.
Simply, taking everything in tow,
Persevering as I always have,
I continue on as long as infinity lasts.

Leviathan

What dwells in waters unknown?
A child's fears, an adult's terrors?
The frigid, deep waters of the abyss,
Reflecting no visible light,
Giving off a blackness that's more terrifying than night.

Grew up swimming as fast as I could to avoid what dwells beneath.
The terrible life threatening image,
That burns the inside of my eyelids as I try to sleep.
The unknown is a frightening beast,
But maybe a perspective change is all I need?

I dive down and submerge myself in the deepest depths I can find.
Holding a rock, sitting isolated in place,
Looking around into nothing.
I can't even see my hand in front of my face.
There is no fear here anymore,
I've left myself vulnerable and nothing has struck me.

The cold temperature forms an almost shell of comfort,
Like this is where I belong,
As if all that matters is my confinement,
To drown out all the noise from within.

All of a sudden, a torrent of water rushes violently past me,
Alerting me to a monstrous presence.

The giant serpent shaped dragon brushes by my body,
Curls around me on the murky, soft detritus ridden floor.
A shark's eye view reveals a spiral with me as the center piece.
It nestles its maw against my side,
The yellow, reptile eye piercing the darkness,
Not just of the lightless depths, but of my soul.

This is my leviathan,

Erik Belmer

This is my water guardian,

As I swim up for breath,
It flaps its wyvern like wings,
And guides me to the top with a ferocious force.
Now relieved from my oxygen deprivation,
It's coarse, yet slippery scales hold me up,
As it rests below my form.

In the newly found light I see the true beauty of this creature.
Its aquamarine fins glistening in the UV rays,
Leathery, double jointed wings that close in for drag,
Rigid, weathered scales showing chips and breaks.

My reflection in the sea shows
This creature is part of me,
Adaptable and cunning.
Fusing the best parts of me,
With everything yet to be.

Slowly taking in new breath,
Sporting a devilish grin,
I dive back in.

The unknown doesn't scare me anymore,
I know what dwells within,
My home, my comfort,
My leviathan, my water guardian,
Within.

Yesterday's Mo(u)rning

We're told not to believe in it
We're told not to try
Love doesn't exist
In this generations blind, dead eyes

There's no morality
No sense of conformity
Just a leave the good behind
Hold up the weak
Fuel false humanity
It's a feral release
Of what humans are meant to be

        I'm not your fucking martyr
        I'm not here to fucking barter
        It's not my life on a funeral pyre
        It's your false ideals on fire

        I'm your replacement
        Genius in your mind
        Puppeteer without strings
        To show you how things are supposed to be

        I'm your fucking lifeline
        I'm your goodnight
        I'm your hopeful wake up
        I'm your dream

        I am love
        That left you cold and alone
        To eventually make this easy

        It's just another morning
        You don't need me
        And I don't need you

Erik Belmer

You're wrong
I still believe
It's better to love
And hope for connection
To arm yourself after rejection
To stare at the sun
Creating your universal reflection

Black Rose

There's a black rose on my dashboard.
It's not a sign of darkness,
Just a sign of decay.
A symbol of love lost,
An acceptance to move on at all cost.

Bury the past,
Return this rose to its home.
Reinstitute the earthly cycle.

Grow, decay, renew,
But keep the memories with you.
That's what makes you true.
Recognizable change,
Of broken thorns,
And petals of organic ash.

That's how nature works,
No need for us to be so rash.
Accept the change,
Be part of a new human path.

Bury the past,
Return this rose to its home.
Reinstitute the earthly cycle,
Until this flower stays its honest color,
A supple, red, flowy hue,
And that's when you know this love is true.

An eternal chance,
For me and you.

Don't Burn The Pages

How do I know it's real this time?
Is it different than before?
Lust and chemicals?

No, not lust at all
Definitely brain chemicals
I feel like I'm high
But there is polarity here
I can't turn away
It's not just me either
But I see you darling
Just like you see me

I let you read the words
I didn't realize until after
That I let you read my soul
The book is open
You can't burn those pages

I've only looked upon you once
I liked what I saw
Cute, charming, funny
So much in a beautiful package
So much more to unwrap

I feel you
Without ever touching you
Don't try to burn the pages
Please

Anxiety

It sits and waits,
At the end of the world.
Parasitically chained to you,
It needs no explanation,
And revels in consternation.

It's not just fear,
It's your subconscious,
It's here to be an ever-present monster.

You think you're going to croak,
Wait on me.
It's not just chest pains,
It's migraines,
Heart palpitations,
And numb extremities.

To make the victim swoon,
Truly it's my desire.
To make you bleed without blood,
To make you worry without reason,
For you to ache without injury.
I am your owner and your master,
I am fear, your daily disaster.

And you think the devil's song is the one,
His name matters not in the fever I run.
I'll make this prison sentence last,
I'll be your present, future and past,
As time warps and loses track.

My name is anxiety,
And you will not know peace.
My name is anxiety,
And you will never sleep.

Erik Belmer

I am the monster of the mind,
The one you choose to deny.

You have no place,
And no time,
The rest of you will soon be mine.

Sparks

It starts as a glance
Progresses to a gaze
Initially an aesthetic process
Transforms with words
Equivocal brain waves
Hold weight for future days

Once you're on the same page
Eyes meet locked together
No sign of breaking away
The sparks fly
Falling in a circular pattern
Encompassing just you and me

The fire in our eyes
Can't be matched
Others would meet their demise
It's me and you darling
With our profound orbitals glued
The floor singed
From the chemical burns
Of our two souls unhinged

That ancient feeling
Awakened from universal symmetry
Hidden away from past you and me
Eerily satisfied by proximity
All others recoil away

Let us dance inside each other's mind
For a second or a lifetime
We'll be just fine

Rogue Clothes

Glossy eyes and a mild headache
Aggressively accosted by my shirt
The smell of you lingers
Like a slap in the face
Another reminder, of the wrong one
It all comes out in the wash

Bad memories should work that way
Just washed away instantly

Instead like loitering ghosts
Waiting for a fix to move on
Masked, but always present
Because time isn't a healing property
Simply a history lesson

(At least this time you learned
Bailed early at the first sign of control
Just a dent in your mental fortitude
As you trudge through the mire
Of siren's and succubus's victims)

Trust me
I listened
I heard it all
I just didn't like the tune

Trust me
My eyes were open
I saw you clearly
I didn't like the picture painted

So, the mire became sand
And sand became stone
The stone became a foothold
And I stand above it all

The Poet

The poet is neither a liar, a thief, nor a fraud.
He is a momentary visionary.

For simply relaying feelings honestly in a moment in time, is not a curse onto others.

It's an explanation of raw emotions,
Wrought with a penchant for words in a linear space of time.
Time is the bastard child here,
Because feelings are fluid based on circumstance.

After party

The sweet summer sprinkle
Wooden boards beneath our feet
Clumsy foot patterns
That brought us together

A dance on a slippery porch
A summary I adore
A touch of our hands and a simple spin
Retract your arms
And let you fall against my skin

Two gleaming pairs of blue eyes, unmatched
Parallel to the black background
Glints of moonlight illuminate our tree line
As the shadows of insignificant humans shift around us
We stay motionless
Our spirits delving into each other's form

Seductive synapse
Electrical relapse
A hop, skip and a jump
Solder the feelings
So we come back to this moment
When we first knew the truth

That not all things are planned
That your perfect design is flawed
That the person you're looking for
Never existed at all
It was a mirrored imperfection
Of your own dream reflection

Bipolar

I hate to see that face
That acceptance of what you lost
That was me, I see it in your awkward glance

You're asking yourself what you're doing here
At your normal spot
Sitting in your own head, looking clinical depressed

Then you wonder what he's doing here
Looking happy, playing it off
Talking to girls he won't ever take home
A fake smile just to get by

Maybe he's not happy, seeing me this way
I guess I'm not ready for his light
I lied; I told him I just wanted to have fun
But damn I think of all of stupid puns
And I can't accept that I'm strung up
On a guy I could have made mine

Fear and anxiety ruined my good time
A chance for a lifetime
The answer I wanted
I was too afraid to make mine

A saving grace in a short race
Should I put this life to waste?
I can't shake this do or don't two-way switch
On which face really commits
It's my disease he accepted openly
He just didn't understand what it truly meant
……I could never be more

Long Forgotten Feelings

It was there all this time
Right in front of you
You always thought she was fine
A hidden gem in a valley of monotony

Do I want to make this girl mine?
She's gorgeous and funny
And makes a rainy day sunny
Her laugh is intoxicating
Her eyes are mesmerizing
Her lips are tantalizing
A sweet viscous smile
That will never let me go senile

She compliments my crazy
It's an apparent acceptance
Our dramatic entrance

She cares and she's real
Can that be a thing?
I'm head over heels
She hit me right in the feels

I ripped down all the spiderwebs
On our staircase descent
Just to make you understand
That I can be that guy for you
I fucking hate spiders, I really do

Just one more look
Just one more quirky smile
That will take me miles
I'll wake up feeling brand new
A sense of hope reissued

Can you be that girl?
At least I'm trying to let you be

Something important to me
And that's new

I'll break down my wall
And start to free fall
Just so you can catch me

Erik Belmer

The Reincarnate

I've waited so long
To see you again
I don't even know what time we're in
But I know it's you, because I feel you
Unmistakable memories buried within
I just have to look in those soulful eyes
Windows that let it all flow back again

I like the nice choice of human you're in
I guess I got lucky
It's not like we actually have a choice
Other than good deeds of past lives
I guess this skin is my prize

It's all superficial though
What matters is we're together
To walk this realm hand in hand
Until our next death separation
Where we play our hand again

Hello, my love
Our karma driven happenstance
Makes this time warp and species dance
More than I can stand

We're back on top
The species so complex
It can shed tears of happiness
Accentuate pain with pleasure
Laugh at the rush of death
Love so hard that there's nothing left
So, you're back in my arms
Synergistic bonds reattached
Our minds entwined
Let us enjoy this planet
While taking care of it this time
So we can be each other's

Without fear of our after form
Let's do it right, so human is our constant
And then I will find you in every life

Memorial

An ironic uprising lies
At the chasm of atrocity
Hope in cleansing form
As water cascades off stone
From etched markings

The souls that once screamed
In pain and anguish
Now mold together
As one reverberating sound

One after another
Drop after drop

The tears of the lost
Form a blanket of comfort
To all who visit
Just sit and listen
It will all become clear

We are not lost forever
We still have something to say
In our wake
We formed a beautiful array
Of sound and symbolism
To remind you, we are one
It's time to change our ways

And So, The World Burns

It's just free electricity
Fuck using it sparingly
I'll use every drop selfishly
The ecosystem can't control free
Because that's what we all are
Dumb walking corpses
Carrying our own torches
Upside down to the ground

And so, the world burns, effortlessly
And so, the word burns, constantly

Walking through flames
All hope is lost
All thoughts are at a cost
When they are made selfishly

Ignorant hands horde and touch
Succumbing those on the front lines
Consternation muddles the mind
As the TV gleams its sadistic smile

And so, the world burns, effortlessly
And so, the world burns, constantly

Those that can't sit, drown
Inner peace is disallowed
In a system that feeds on greed and instability

As addiction becomes the chapter
Corpses become the pages
Blood becomes the script
The publication date 2000 and when?

And so, the world burns, effortlessly
And so, the world burns, constantly

Absolution

Slowly he judges her eyes,
Looking for any sign of rejection.
Because his minds racing,
There is hesitation,
However,
She has nothing but acceptance.
Glossy whites mixed with vibrant green,
Exposing only truth.

His hands dip and hold steady,
As the small of her back relaxes.
The air nonchalantly synchronizes,
As two hearts beat in step.

His first move but not his last.
As the earth burns in the far distance,
He knows it's best to go out,
With love and anticipation coating the air.
For the next life is their only bet.

The slow pull of her form,
Brings their lips paper thin,
And the lover dives in.
A strong eternal caress, not in fear,
But in absolution.

For she is the one,
In this life or the next.

So, fire and radiation rain down,
Making ash and bone,
Meld together,
In a universal array.
Lovers together,
In every single way.

Dystopian Senses

The foggy doldrums of senses mulled.
Like a bright hazy star,
The ominous backdrop,
Of a bleak encompassing gray shroud.

There is no smoke,
Thus, there is no fire,
Just lost desire.
A path unwound,
As you try to find trees,
That no longer fill the ground.

No early morning birds,
No crickets in summer's heat.
Just tepid earth,
And organic carbon litter the ground.

No breath will be taken.
For radiation stagnates the air,
Silent and noxious,
The looming human killer,
That sight cannot unveil.

Dusty books and crumbled buildings,
Forgotten knowledge, ready to be picked,
By those daring enough,
To rebuild the lost ways,
From ignorance and tyranny,
That has no bounds.

Careful though.
For knowledge is power,
And in the wrong hands,
The dystopian senses will rebound.

Vice Grip

It's coming to a close
I know this pain can't continue
I'm already bleeding out internally
My bodies a torrent of crimson shreds

The black fatality carrier pulled up
The chauffeur put the window down
Beckoned me to the passenger seat
I sat down cautiously
I looked him in his sunken eyes
As he reached out for my hand
With menacing, soft, white bones
Protruding in the moonlights gleam

Accepted
Arm wrestling death
The torquing bones of contention
Vice grip of an afterlife
But it's not my time

A stubborn refusal
Based upon true loves concept
This Leo's only prize
And maybe his demise

I'll make a deal with any immortal
To come back to this hellish world
To fucking find her
I'll fucking find her

I didn't sit in misery blissfully
Or walk the line of strife blindly
To leave this broken planet
Without feeling it's only saving grace
A love locked soul connection

I broke that motherfucker's arm
Took his head with his own scythe
Peeled out of the drive way
And came back to life

I don't remember what price I paid
When I was stuck in the white haze
Maybe I sold my soul
Maybe I got lucky
But I'll find that girl
So Death, go fuck thee

Hank Moody

Victim to feelings
Protagonist to error

The writer drowns his sorrow
Brown, black or white
Women or booze
He doesn't discriminate
As long as he avoids the now

Some days he will write
Some days he will slander

If the now becomes apparent
He's not afraid
...He's too particular
How do you relate?
The words craft a story if you read between the lines
The real question is will anyone ever see?

Inadequate, hurt, misused
Narcissistic, cruel, manipulative

The writer's ploy
The read between lines
The writer's truth

He sees you
He sees him
Double edged sword with no intent
Sow the sorrow
Or reap the maleficent
It's all held within the ink in the pen

The Note

You're wearing a new necklace
The kind that is expensive
Small, heart shaped with tiny diamonds
I asked because it had only been two months

You told me
"It was from someone who thought you were worth more than you are"
That kind of self-loathing I understand

That's probably why you're out having drinks with me
Because I understand
And I'll take you home and fuck you
The way you like to be fucked
Treat you like you matter
Like you're a human, with all your flaws
Like you're a human, with all your beauty

That's why you left me a note that said I love you

Arm's Length

Our fire is not one of red, nor yellow.
There is no orange intense hue,
Just a white blinding light,
Like magnesium that burns bright.

The time lapse is minimal at best.
A couple of lover's photos,
Smiles of relationships upstart,
Pure ecstasy caught in time.
Each other's lifeline?
Or each other's obstacle?
A mystery novel with no end,
Because you don't hold the futures pen.

Self-sabotage seems likely,
As your own worst enemy rears his head,
The mirrored reflection of perfection.
Lecheries connection is half the battle,
Arts and creation the quarter,
Adrenaline activities the missing key,
Maybe she's just not the girl for me.

Is this the same mistake?
Letting someone in,
And closing the gates,
As the second side encroaches,
On the naivety of your hope.

Arm's length becomes decision,
Assessment and revision.
A learning tool and defense,
Against poisoned pages,
And chapters already written.
I refuse to be my own victim.

The Game

Words unspoken,
As the clocks turn,
And I sit by the phone,
Predicting why you're distant.

Wait too long?
Wait not long enough?
Overeager or careless?

Nice guy or bad guy?
Which side is best?

But really, it's the game I detest.
Feelings exposed,
Rather than dormant.
They shine vibrantly,
Sun like, as the radiation pours over.
Most shy away from the light.
I'm tired of the vampires anyways,
They've been sucking me dry since birth.
Give me the purist,
The girl to cup it in her hands,
To drink the draught,
With an eager smile.
For my soul,
It needs that counterpart.

Ugly World

The world showed me its ugly face
...Again

I laughed, the kind of sick laugh
That any random person would raise their eyebrows in concern at
Like your cackling straight up to the gods
Internally emanating the words
Fucking try me motherfuckers

The kind of fed up feeling where you pound your chest like an ape
Punch yourself in the jaw
Headbutt the wall
To prove you can take it
...But can you??

You're clearly breaking
But the gods already know that
They made this story
At least you're convinced you can shape it

Christmas Present

A twinge of hope
A slight discourse
Feelings out of the blue
She came clad in black
The nerdy, adorable girl
That used words to whip and whirl

On the day of presents
You were my gift
Of the future times we can never omit
Memories I'll never remit

Late night calls
And chilly sprawls
That's a wintership

Like ice on the windows
Removing sight from the road
Serene auras of two guided our path

Quaint, little towns in the mountains
Composed of breweries and churches
Allowed the winding roads to our place
Where time is just our cute space

The holiday of hearts is upon us
I've glimpsed inside yours
And cast a glimmer of mine

So point your arrow
Aim true and release
The target is what's inside of you

A makeshift poem
A romantic tome
Story book paths
That become interwove

Erik Belmer

Darling, I have all night
To sit and listen
You're the gorgeous girl
The girl I've been missing

Poisoned Sands

It's the most malicious thing in the world
Caustic to our entire being
It grates against our skin
It corrodes our soul
It shackles our spirit

Initially from morning to evening
From night to day
It erected daily structure
Until we gave it three heads
Present, future, and past
Buildings razed and lives lost
This lesson comes at a cost

We named it
We created its hands
And counted its lifespan
Hieroglyphs, books and doomsday clocks
We've all been given a finish before a start

The idea is a stopwatch for mortals
Without an end in sight
Fear envelops its meaning
As it gorges itself
From the back of our minds
For ideas carry a burden
And venomous sands will churn
Creating our hourglass shaped urn

Stray from the path
Stay young at heart
Impervious to stagnation
Rage wild amongst conformity
Fluoresce against the drab ensemble
Unchain your spirit

Erik Belmer

For to name time is poison
And humans need not play
Under the sink of the unknown

The Glass Remembers

A tremored hand unveils nerves,
Nerves you wish you didn't have.
In your heart you knew it was over,
You were just too craven.
Honesty always waivers internally,
As others always pay the price.
Always on your time.

Alas, that's where the guilt dwells.
A quick change of thought occurs,
As you catch her mischievous eyes,
Those green seductive gems.

As she guides your path,
Hands clasped with a tug of authority,
The carnival lights swirl around,
Making the drink seem more potent,
As colors blend and weave.
It seems the funhouse is your destination.
Pun unintended, you chuckle to yourself.

Knowing by sense,
The house of mirrors is your hideaway.
A quick pull of your arm and a slight push of her body,
You fall into her against the glass.
She slowly brushes your lips,
Absolving all guilt with lecherous arousal.
Up against the glass fully entwined,
As your shapes shift and form in the mirrors game.

The glass remembers the end,
Is also the beginning.
As long as it doesn't crack.
Spiderwebs tend to catch,
Best not to end up in a trap.

Scenario Brain

Mysterious pondering thoughts
Think you're in a race
Then a swift crisscross
And you're back to the start
Of working backwards
Solving puzzles and predicting disaster

Scenario brain is a cosmic joke
To the feeble creatures accepting their mundane lives
Only you can entertain feelings so omniscient

Hate me because I'm better
Hate me because I'm wiser
Love me because it's not your curse
Accept me, because it fucking hurts

When you can never be satisfied
Some days you wish you'd wake up clueless
Just so you can take a breath
And let the gears rest

That won't happen so you sit and grin
So devilishly
Oh so, devilishly
Wicked smile as you watch and learn
Mannerisms, actions, thoughts
All predictable
Oh so, predictable

Hate me because I'm better
Hate me because I'm wiser
Love me because it's not your curse
Accept me, because it fucking hurts

For all my worth
Figuring out which road to take
Was never in my design

Cupid's Carrying A 45

Just a manic brain
Hell bent on disaster
Sewing chaos in my wake

Jump in for the ride
Or sit in ashes I displace

Adorations Fall

Hello, my name is Autumn,
I'm not just a leaf that blows away effortlessly.
I'm a girl that changes color,
Right in front of your eyes,
It's not just another disguise.

It's not a reptile skill,
Just my emotions on a train line.
You see everything as a blur,
In real time though it's a cure.
To see a myriad of colors,
And a world rediscovered as wonder.

I broke the book The Giver,
To give you all a better picture,
Of what life should be,
An effortless symphony.

Acid trips aren't even for me,
It's just using your eyes acceptably,
Observation skills and imagery thrills.
I'm your muse of different hues,
See me, feel me, use me.
I'm your shifting picture,
The wonder undiscovered.
A cure to this love sick race.
Just adore my beauty.
Let everything slip away.

The In-Between

It's a morbid, astral curiosity
Your sadness lamented
By spirits attached to your skin
You dove into the other side
Rejected
Placed back on earth
To walk again with a lesson to learn
...Too bad it's hidden within

I don't remember my time there
But I came back changed
For better or worse
Only time will tell

I feel different, I think different
Dancing with death
Leaves secret scars
Touched by the hand
Yet, I still live

It's a weird longing for the unknown
That's been left within
Unraveling hidden truths of the universe
You'll never win
I understand, even though I don't
Don't fuck with the astral plane
Clouded footholds
Empty sounds
Until within gives sight

Find purpose in aimless direction?
Or enjoy the amenities presented?
Which pill will you take?
The red?
The blue?

Erik Belmer

Neither, stuck between the present and the past
Infinitesimal mind and weak bones
Walk on and leave that realm alone

The Passed by Looking Glass

                        It's an empathy based sort of disdain,
              I see you; I feel you, but I don't know your pain.

                                 What happened to you?
        Why are you so disheveled, and left to the open weather?
                                  Was it the wheelchair,
              Or the fact that someone didn't care about you?
Did they leave you out here all alone, estranged from your home?

                 Then as if he used his mind to speak to you.

He said,
    "Young man,

My thoughts are miles,
My eyes are canyons,
My voice a vestige, whispers memories,
Of a life that I used to know.
All sealed in place,
Hidden behind my face.

I've seen empty beer cans pile,
And dope sicken people smile,
What is this hell, where I watch people prove self-exile?

With open eyes and no tongue to speak,
The only thing to shield me from this world is the blanket covering me.
I don't know where it came from, or who tried to comfort me.
I still believe there is a universal power left for me.

I've seen things no man should see,
Countless beatings to the weak,
Even men dying in the street.
Pavement cracks mixing with congealed blood,
Leaving a flat surface of red and black.
Only to be trod over by the unaware,

Leaving no trace of the men once there.

I've heard things that no man should hear.
Lustful, fake humans cheating themselves,
Of the happiness they already have.
Kissing each other seductively as they say goodbye.
Setting up future "meetings", as they recap their affair.
Insidiously smiling at the devil within one another,
Leaving their significant others alone, at home, under their bed covers.

It happens all too frequently,
When they think you're not watching or listening.
Or maybe they just don't care.
Clearly, I couldn't stop them,
Or come to anyone's defense,
I'm just a mute in a wheelchair.

I just sit here and watch the human race crumble all around me.
Wasted lives, corrupt intentions and selfish transgressions.
The worlds a broken shell of its former wealth,
Transcending into hell itself.

My thoughts are miles,
My eyes are canyons,
My voice a vestige, whispers memories,
Of a life that I used to know.
All sealed in place,
Hidden behind my face.

Is euthanasia a reprieve to life?
Can it bury the pain,
And give me my relief?

I'm old and my family is gone,
But I'm still living on.
Please euthanize me,
Give me some sort of reprieve."

In lieu of your reprieve,
May your soul find peace,
May your heart find solace.

Saturn Rising

Saturn Rising.
Four white lighters in my pocket,
Trying to bring the uprising.
I'm 27 trying to make it to 28,
Trying to make it in every dead hero's wake.

No path, no guidance.
Just an astrological prophecy,
Based on the deceased.

Genealogy and oddity,
These words haunt me,
As maturity crosses with adolescence.

Can we make it, when half of us fake it?
Do the stars even care if we can take it?
Orion's utility belt,
Ursa Major's claws,
Leo's fangs,
Sagittarius's arrow,
Can this shit save us?

Or if we ignore the skies with a pessimistic disguise,
And a selfish glint in our eyes,
Can that shit save us?

What the fuck will save us?
Maybe only destiny knows.

She's no stripper up on a pole,
Or a random girl that will save your soul,
Just an idea that makes you question what makes you whole.

Open the path into the darkness,
Listen to the noise,
That will guide you walking straight up through the hidden door.

And when they ring will you take the call?
Or will you say fuck the stars,
I'll wait for the rest to unfold it all?

Erik Belmer

My Pictures Face Up

5 years down
There is still no shake in the earth
No resounding voice that carries
Just an empty, vacant space
An open cavity I can't erase

Your picture is blurred
My memory is hazy
Walking in a daydream
Who's going to wake me

Technologies freeze frame
Is our only discourse now
What was never said becomes endless
A simple smile and a playful laugh
Those are the memories that matter
The quick glimpses of before that shatter

Choosing between respect and defense
The grey area, between integrity and lies
The questions that make most falter
My bedrock, my structure, my alma mater

Life dealt the cards
You taught me how to beat the dealer
Ironically, you're the one that folded
And in the end
A human's hands are his bed
Deeds and actions seal fate
And suicide is a deep drink to take

There's blood on the floor
A shower curtain crumpled
And regret fills the air
A wallet with my picture lays in place
It's face up
I'm face up

I'm the last thing you saw
As you tried to staunch the wounds
Tried to save your soul
It wasn't enough
So, the blood runs out
Through the floorboards
…The blood runs down
As your life force soils the ground

I'll see you again
Just not in this dimension
The one that harbors your regret and hate

My dominion
Where you don't control my fate
Where I can tear down misery's gates
Into a life learning from your mistakes

Family Mirror

After you shake off the booze,
Fingers run through flowy hair,
Water cupped to accentuate morning.

The mirror stares back.
Are you going to do it?
Are you just like him?

You spill the water over your face,
As if you could erase that train of thought.

No, you were never like him,
Statistics voice consternation,
Like father like son.
But your soul knows better.
There may be an answer in death,
And you may chase it,
Laugh in the face of it,
And revel in its proximity.

But never at your own hands,
It's not fair to everyone else.

6th Month Killer

It's black under the sliver of moon
When the familiar feeling strikes
Slow, cold flow of liquid
Congealing in your veins
Freezing blood makes its way to the heart
It's the 6th month killer
Tearing your life apart

Hollow solitude forms a saving grace
The darkest blanket covering your pain
All sound reverberates
To empty ears
Never in the same plane

Truly alone you fight the crushing weight
And conjoin with the darkness
This is your strength
This is your fate
Always fighting
For a reason you're in this place

Nothing lasts forever
But memories speak volumes
And you always tried hardest
To shape destiny in your hands
Molding predetermined events

Will you ever find comfort?
Will you ever find your home?
Is this the warrior's life,
Fighting on into the eternal unknown?

Winters Caress

Hello my name is winter,
I'm not a simple flake that melts away.
I'm a foundation of vibrant white,
A mask of purity,
Draped over human fingers etched into the land.

I make time freeze,
As heavenly shapes coat the landscape.
The wind whipped dance ebbs and flows,
Creating a stillness within.
As all noise molds into a uniform caress.
I absorb all pain and sorrow,
All distress,
Allowing you humans to fluoresce.

I will take your breath away,
Instilling new found purpose,
As cold life drains from my lips,
To your chest.
I'm the girl you like best,
I offer direction, strength, and comfort
As I wrap you in my white dress.

As I lay my white sheets,
Over your trafficked streets,
Countless avenues arrive,
But never the same path.
For I am winter, the girl that allows,
You humans to move on,
To never regress,
To keep trying to be your best.

Second Choice

You think you're second
And that I tricked you
Babe, you have every right
I wasn't honest with my love plight

The purest form of a toxin
It forces my hand
It bends my will
It's my disguise and my muse
My condolences for the ruse

My spirit stands on deaths door
My soul in chains, stands on trial
My heart is a viscous prosecutor
My mind is an ironclad defendant
But damn, love is the sharpest weapon

I painted you the victim
In my escape attempt
Running will never lead to resolve
So turn and face your devil
Sever your corrupted heart strings
Once and for all

You are no longer second, nor are you first
You're the epitome of redemption
The one to tell me how it really is
The beautiful, steadfast woman to take the call
Strong enough to withstand the toxic pall

Titles and unnecessary words stand still
As time takes control
I see you; I know you
Whether forever, or right now
I'll gladly take a bow

Earned Throne

When they throw the dirt on your face
I'll be the one to take your hand
Your stoic escort, built out of hate

I'll rip the gates of hell open
And shuffle you into the queue
So you can make your final descent
Punishment from deeds of your own accord

I'll stand eagerly watching
Making sure there's no escape

No lie will save you
No god will answer you
Just a devil's dance of deliverance
For the crimes you committed
Slander, abuse, manipulation

Welcome to your eternal puppet show
You're no longer the master
Just a feeble pawn
Serving a permanent, daily disaster

Thank you for the character defamation
Now accept your seat in hell
The barbed, thorned, razorblade encompassed chair
Where you will forever dwell

I couldn't break your evil spell
I owned the lie, I live the lie
I've waited so long for retribution
I was waiting on time itself
Not borrowed, simply karma driven

When we reach this close
And you're where you belong
No joy will overwhelm me

Cupid's Carrying A 45

No smile will cross my face
Just a satisfactory look
Knowing you can't hurt anyone else
Living in your new found place

This is a sad day of remorse
You couldn't atone on your own
Now take your fucking throne

Heart of the Run

It all comes down to
The Heart of the Run

Location change
To stay the pain
Faces in the street
Eyes that creep
Adrenal glands maxed
Senses taxed

So, memories relapse
Like biting your tongue
To taste bitter blood
Just a reminder
Just a reminder
That cursory pounding
In your chest
Likes pain the best

Your face is the reminder
Until I get caught up on the next
So, the beat keeps going
The Heart of the Run
It drums in your chest

Succubus in My Mind

You earned my trust
I handed you the keys
The tomes on the wall
In the corridors of my mind's labyrinth
Speak of every ounce of me

You took that knowledge
And used it maliciously
Each word, another crack
In the foundation of me

As your whisperings poison my ears
Succubus in my mind says
"You will know fear"

You brought me down
Toppling over in ruins
All alone, on my own
Chained only to you
Dependency is what you wanted
Weak and lifeless
Not willing to put up a fight
Settling night after night

As you rope me in again
With your luscious kisses
And supple form unclad
Legs spread wide
Just begging for me inside
Time after time, I lose more of my mind

You chose the wrong man
You don't know me

You don't know me
This is my place of strength
Alone at the bottom

Erik Belmer

With nothing else but survival
This is where I thrive
Succubus in my mind
You will know fear

And soon you will miss my presence
As I come and go and you lose control
You will crave my essence
As the bottom becomes the top
Inversion becomes the narrative

You're the one that can't live without me
My form, my skill, my passion
Succubus meet your incubus
I hold the cards now
Because, survival that's my only incentive

Queen of Disarray

You're my writers block
The shackles grasping my brain
Taking away my peace
Leaving me in cognitive decay
I haven't written anything in four damn months

Your eyes burn the page
Your thoughts blank my mind
Your touch stays my hand
Your words freeze the ink

It's history's oblivion
You as the chapter
You're the queen of disarray
Cadavers of the weak lie in your wake

I'm not the weak
I'm not your drowned victim
I'm the scarred
Your name on my tongue
Your image on my skin
But I still live

With five fingers to the page
I write your name

With five fingers to the page
I write your name

There is no shake
There is no quiver
Just concise marks
…A black scripture
…A warning to all

The Unborn

I altered the timeline,
I spat in the face of the gods.
I chose death for the unborn,
The beautiful queen now forlorn.

I cannot stop the tears,
I cannot quell your fears,
But I've given you years.

Escape the fate.
That's what we did,
I just had to be the bad guy,
That flicked the switch.

False promises,
And biological clocks.
Those aren't the keys,
To a child's upstart.

Those are his grievances,
And his death sentence.
To be born to parents who wanted family,
But didn't work universally.

It was in our hearts,
But never in our stars,
And that's the hardest part.

Some days it haunts me,
Others it fuels my ire.
Did we meet purposely?
What was the point,
Of our cataclysmic atrocity,
When all we have left is grief and animosity?
We will never know.
The unborn's demise,

Leaves a permanent stain.
It means no coming back for you and I.

Erik Belmer

Our Little Monster

We didn't even know
We were never prepared
Looming, ominous figurehead
Of everything we couldn't seer

This is our little monster
Trapped in the basement
Grotesque, gluttonous appetite
Of all our angst and strife
It gets fat and happy
Just waiting
Just waiting
For its fucking time to strike

Only took a year
Door blasted off its hinges
Apartment tattered in shreds
Broken tiles and scorched floors
This is our full-grown monster
Armed to the teeth, with all our fears
Ready to see us kill each other
As he whispers in our ears

We created this
We burned the red flags
We taunted the gods
We stayed together

We fought, cried and bled
Told ourselves this was just
But now he's here
Our fucking monster
Tearing our life apart

Can we destroy it?
Obliterate its presence?
Not together

No
Not together
No

We must leave this house in shreds
And continue our worldly venture, alone
Only then can we return our monster to its bed

Dishes

I thought about you today
For the first time, in a long time
I thought about what it would be like
To be in a house with you again

Then I remembered your order
My "inconsistencies"
The anger in your eyes
Like I was spiting you

Who ever knew
Dishes are to be done systematically:
Cups first
Then forks and knives
Spoons after that
Bowls and plates next
Pans last
No sponge
Until after your hand washes away the food

A sponge isn't supposed to be dirty
It's supposed to stay pristine in the rack
Until it withers down, slowly
So you can crumble it in your hands
...Doing the dishes just isn't enough

Banana Pancakes

Regaining my place,
As the flashback ends,
The bite waiting on the fork.
The pancakes taste stale,
All the flavors:
Cinnamon, vanilla, banana.
They're all present.
Yet in my reverie,
A pure flash of her beautiful face,
And the mornings we used to share.
Memories that warm,
...Equally haunt,
Lingering even after 6 months.
So I eat unsatisfied this morning.
I don't even drink my coffee the same way,
I had to change that.
Had to try something.
Because it's not healthy,
Or maybe it is?
Maybe I'm just too caring?
I'll try not to wander next time.
I know your mind won't.
I'll try to be better to myself.

Different Exits

Parallel sidewalks
A sob that extends miles
Your gait surpasses mine
As you drip melancholy from your eyes

I'm also walking alone this New Year's Eve
The rose I was holding
Dropped to the ground as I left the bar
Yellow, beautiful and vibrant
Pouring its spectrum on dull footholds
That made me forlorn
Where are your tears from?

You're whisked away
As I sit in my head

I almost slipped and fell
The funny thing is
The contortion from my abs in midair
Safely landed me away from the puddle
On my hands I laughed
...Cackled actually

Staring at the water
It may have altered my night
One simple contortion
One sureness within
My agility and physical prowess

Cheers from random strangers erupted
New friends born from that moment
Weaved into drinks and philosophy talks

Then a text from the cute bartender
I forgot I had her number from months ago

It was nice to wake up holding someone

Remember
Parallel roads travel the same direction
But they also have different exits

Fingerprint

I licked my phone to unlock it
Out of anger
Because I pressed the button three times
Still my fingerprint was unworthy
So I used my ire to show technology up

You don't like me motherfucker
Well too god damn bad
I'm here to piss on your parade
And short circuit the generation
A little saliva never hurt anyone
And technology listened

Spit works wonders

Touch Topography

His hands glide over her lithe form.
Slowly his fingertips distinguish,
Every dip, crest and curve,
Of his most beautiful muse.

That sly half-hidden smile eclipses her face,
From the corner of her lips.
Born from letting her guard down,
Implications or not, she told him not to stop.

Subconsciously his hands weave,
A mental map of her tone, sexy being,
As if he could see the midi-chlorians of her makeup.

Eternalized in memory.
Not only in sight,
But in touch and aura.
The latter being the key.
Now he sees her and feels her,
Wherever she may be.

A Poem Goodnight

The heat from the night
The soft hum of a fan
Your skin sits hot
Devoid of sweat
But longing with anticipation
For the color of blushing
Doesn't simply disappear
It's a kiss on your soul
And that will last
Until the kiss on your lips
Is a worthy mirror

So, for tonight
We shall say goodnight
As anticipation carries our dreams
To the slumbered halls
Of what remains to be seen

Photo By Erik Belmer

About The Poet

Erik Belmer is a poet based out of Denver Colorado. He is a professional bartender that loves inventing cocktails when he isn't using his creativity for poetry. His job allows him to travel and explore new places. He often chooses areas to live that are accessible to the outdoors where he is most at home as an avid hiker and skier. Erik was born in North Conway, New Hampshire and grew up in New England.